How to Analyze People

A Psychologist's Guide to Human Behavior, Body Language, Personality Types and Reading People

(Learn the key to instantly uncover what people think and feel just by observing them)

Patrick Lightman

D1562549

Table of Contents

Introduction

If I were to ask you, "What is the single most important skill that will give in an edge over others in a personal, professional and social set-up?", what would your answer be? Think about it carefully. We are social creatures and our ability to succeed in life pretty much depends on our ability to understand people. Throughout our lives, a majority of our time is spent in interaction with people (unless you live in a cardboard box or rabbit hole) and developing new associations. If you were to ask me for the single biggest vital survival and success skill in today's world, it would undoubtedly be the art of analyzing people.

How will you figure out if a prospective employee is a perfect fit for your organizational values and goals? How will you determine if the attractive new lady/man you fancy will be a positive and inspiring long-term mate? How will you identify if a potential client is worth doing business with? How will you cut winsome deals with the right business partners and associates?

How will you forge rewarding business connections at networking events? The master key to all of the above lies in your ability to analyze people, identify their personality, recognize how they think and feel, and above all, communicate in a relevant or appropriate manner based on their personality or behavior.

What is it that primarily drives and motivates people? What is the main personality type? What does their body language reveal about their subconscious thoughts? When you learn to analyze people and identify their fundamental personality type and their thought patterns, you can communicate with them in a more effective and meaningful manner.

When you have the ability to analyze people's behavior and personality, you have an edge when it comes to adapting your own words and actions to develop a winsome rapport with the other person, thus forming more productive and fulfilling interpersonal relationships or professional associations. Well, analyzing people isn't just vital for FBI sleuths but also for regular, everyday people to form more beneficial connections.

Learning to analyze people is one of the most effective and sharpest skills one can develop in today's fast-paced world where there is no escaping the importance of forming new connections and constantly interacting with people in a frenzied pace. The power to tune in to obvious and subtle clues people give out all the time will equip you with the super power to deliver a message more persuasively or convincingly to a person. When you understand how people think and feel, you'll deliver a message in a manner that is suitable for their thought patterns and actions, thus minimizing the chances of misunderstanding.

You will wield greater control over a conversation or enhance your negotiation skills. People who possess the ability to analyze and read others make for more empathetic friends, partners, employer and leaders. You'll be a razor-sharp businessman and negotiator. As a salesperson or business development person, you'll know exactly what your customer or client wants, which will help boost your sales figures. The scope for conflict-ridden situations will reduce when you understand other people's limitations and structure your communication to suit them.

In short, the skill of reading or analyzing people will determine the quality of relationships you enjoy in life. When you master the tips, techniques and strategies for reading people, you know what to look for while attempting to understand them. What are the unspoken things that are given away by their body language? What does their choice of words reveal about people's personality and attitudes? What is their essential character or personality type? How can you tell if someone is telling the truth or resorting to deception? How can you tell if someone is just being themselves or pretending to be something they clearly aren't?

Monthly glossies have done a lot of disservice to the art of analyzing people by reducing it to pop quizzes such as "What your favorite food says about you" or "What does your favorite lipstick shade reveal about your persona?" It isn't as trivial as marketers or glossy editors have us believe. Analyzing people is about delving into people's minds and understanding their words, thoughts, actions and behavior through psychology-driven principles. It is a comprehensive and deep study that has several factors involved.

Much as you'd like to believe, your favorite fragrance doesn't say much about your personality. It can be highly entertaining and addictive but isn't even remotely accurate. To be a star people analyzer, you need plenty of practice, and the ability to decode personalities.

Though this is a highly intensive field of study involving dynamics of psychology, human behavior, social skills and more, in this book I am packing the most concise, practical and actionable tips that will get you started with reading people. These techniques can be applied just about anywhere, from your workplace to personal relationships to social life. The sky is the limit when you develop the ability to understand people and influence them using this understanding.

According to research, the ability to analyze people can help us predict the outcome of a negotiation correctly in around 80 percent of all instances. Doesn't that give you an edge when it comes to steering a negotiation in the right direction?

However, let's get started with some valuable fundamental people analyzing rules that will help you set you on the path for being an ace people reader.

Humans are invariably wired throughout primitive times to interact with each other via subconscious signals. Sometimes, people may appear to be happy and content on the face of it, but deep inside their subconscious mind they may harbor feelings of resentment, frustration and disappointment. When you learn to watch out for these clues, you can reach out to people more effectively.

What is a person's primary instinct or gut feeling? What we refer to as our gut feeling or instinct is nothing but our ability to latch on to specific clues that a person transmits at a subconscious level.

When a person smiles, our smile muscles are reflexively triggered at a more subconscious level. Therefore, when someone smiles at us, we smile instinctively in return. Human brains are created to capture clues that are not apparent to the conscious mind. For instance, think about the time when a person was behaving in a pleasant and positive manner, yet you experienced a strong sense of discomfort while dealing with them. This is because our minds are wired to latch on to subconscious signals.

It may be something about the person's body language, including high blood pressure, faster heart beat, increased palpitations, sweating and more that our mind catches at a more subconscious level that gives us the feeling that something isn't quite right. This explains why sometimes you just don't like some people even when you don't know them well enough to identify their personality.

Chapter One: Human Psychology Basics Decoded

If you track the human evolutionary pattern, you will understand that our brains are wired to conduct accurate readings about our thoughts, actions and behavior. In the absence of language in primitive ages, how did human beings communicate with each other? They communicated through the medium of tone, voice, expression, gestures, postures, signs and other non-verbal mediums. This implies that the skill of reading people already exists within us. It simply needs to be fine-tuned at a conscious level to help us form more productive and fulfilling relationships.

Everyone from trial attorneys to detectives to salespersons to employers can use people analyzing skills to their advantage. Did you know that high-end car salespersons are trained to peep inside their prospective customer's cars to understand their customers better and strike a rapport with them through small talk? If a salesperson sees a golf kit in the back seat of the car, they'll start a conversation about how they enjoy playing golf over the weekends or about a recent golf championship.

Then trial attorneys will attempt to decode where the jury is swinging simply by observing non-verbal clues offered by the jurors while witnesses, officials or the defendant is being cross examined in the stands. They will also brief their clients about maintaining a body language that generally gives out a positive overall impression about him or her to jurors. This can mean eliminating all non-verbal clues that reveal deception or trickery.

Also, when you learn to analyze people, you view them in a more objective and non-judgmental manner. You will also learn to pick up on clues that reveal deception or untruthful behavior. Let us take an example where people try to manipulate you or get what they want using false flattery. When you master the art of reading people, you will be able to determine if people truly feel those compliments from within or they are simply resorting to fake flattery to get what they want. This helps you protect yourself against other people's vested interests.

Here are some amazing advantages of being a people analyzer:

- You are able to enjoy more fulfilling and rewarding interpersonal relationships, thus reducing the pain of unsuitable relationships. You don't want to kiss a thousand frogs to find that one prince/princess, do you?

- It saves you the time, energy and effort of eliminating toxic people and dealing with only those who match

14

your own objectives, values and expectations. People who sap your energy can be shown the door.

- The ability to analyze people can save you tons of money and hours by hiring employees that are a right fit for your organization.

- As a partner or employer, you can tell when people are being deceitful in a relationship or during an interview. You can select a long-term partner who matches not just your own personality but also your values, personality, behavioral traits and more. It will help you weed out dates whose objectives and expectations do not match your own.

- Analyzing people makes you a more power-packed leader. You'll understand your team's goals, motivations, triggers and much more, which can be effectively leveraged for optimizing their performance. This may lead to greater productivity and overall job satisfaction. Learning to read people can be your highway to professional success.

- It is a vital skill when it comes to carrying out negotiations and sales deals. When you figure out how a person prospective client, business associate or customer is thinking, it is simpler to divert the negotiation to your advantage. For instance, if the other party's body language and other non-verbal clues communicate that they are happy with the negotiation terms, yet they ask for a better deal, you know you have to stick your ground because they are simply trying their luck now. Once you realize they are already sold, you won't make any further concessions.

- Reading people helps you fine tune your own verbal and non-verbal communication for creating a dazzling first impression. It helps you package yourself exactly as you want to create more beneficial connections and relationships. You can position yourself as a genuine, credible, friendly and authoritative individual based on the situation by sending the right verbal and non-verbal clues.

- Your empathy factor increases, and you are able to understand people or reach out to them in troubled times more effectively to form more productive interpersonal relationships.

- You increase your chances of performing well at job interviews by sending the right verbal and non-verbal signals to recruiters. You know how to create the right impression by communicating the values, characteristics and ideals that are appropriate for a specific organization or role.

- Tuning in to other people's body language and verbal communication skills makes you an effective speaker. When you gather clues for your audience's body language, you know exactly what they are thinking or feeling about what you're saying. Are they bored, inspired or suspicious about what you are saying? Do they disagree with what you are saying? This will help you quickly change and adapt your speech to evoke a more favorable response. You will be able to say the right things to strike a chord with your audience and persuade them. As a speaker, you'll discover a common ground for connecting with your audience for better results.

- Your chances of electing leaders, politicians and influencers with the right vision will increase when you learn to understand people's motives through their body language, personality, voice and words. Learn to identify traits that make for a powerful and positive influencer such as integrity, authority, generosity, empathy and more. You will be able to recognize people who truly care about others from those who display vested interests for grabbing power.

People are much like onions. They have multiple personality layers that have to be peeled off to glimpse into their real personality characteristics. Some layers of your personality are apparent, while others are inconspicuous. Sometimes, even we are unable to figure out who we really are because we seem like such a bundle of contradictions to ourselves.

A people analyzer or reader can quickly decipher an individual's personality through several attributes, including what he or she does in their spare time. For example, if you inquire what a person does in their spare time and they reveal they participate in community drives, volunteering activities or contribute to church initiatives, you know they are philanthropic, magnanimous or community conscious. Similarly, if a person says they love partying endlessly or watching television in their free time, they may be low on ambition or seek quick gratification. The point is, even something as seemingly trivial as what a person does in his or her spare time can reveal his or her personality.

Theories of Human Behavior

Classical Conditioning

Classical Conditioning is a popular psychological theory through which people learn by pairing behavior as stimuli and response to the stimuli. This principle is used for training animals too. Don't you reward your dog with a treat each time it fetches the ball? In the pet's mind, fetching is closely associated with treats or rewards, so it invariably learns that it has to fetch the ball if wants to be rewarded with a treat.

All through our life as human beings, classical conditioning helps shape our behavior. As babies, we come to associate crying with being fed and kept clean. Students learn that studying consistently and dedicatedly gets you good grades. Thus, classical conditioning influences our behavior and acts throughout our lives. We learn to respond to a specific stimuli in a particular manner. It is one of the main factors when it comes to determining an individual's behavior.

Human Behavior and Physiology

According to research, people have peculiar physical reactions to certain stimuli that are valuable when it comes to analyzing them. These principles are usually used in the area of criminal psychology to understand how criminals think and what drives them to commit crimes. With the help of biometric technology investigators attempt to identify if the suspect's thoughts are in sync with their actions.

This combination of psychological and physiological techniques is powerful for analyzing the underlying motives of human behavior. The human body undergoes specific physiological reactions when a person is misleading or lying. The reaction can be standalone clues or a combination of dilated pupils, increase in heart rate, greater palpitations, sweating and twitching toes. Physiology or non-verbal clues can help you analyze a person more accurately, though much like other people analyzing theories, it can never be fool proof.

Experiences and Human Behavior

While certain psychologists are of the opinion that our behavior is directly determined by genetics or heredity, others believe that it is a summation of all our experiences since birth. They are of the opinion that our immediate environment or the experiences we undergo in our immediate environment mold our behavior. For example, if a person experiences constant marginalization or prejudice on account of their class or race, they may grow up to despise wealth or seemingly superior races. They may empathize with the oppressed.

Similarly, if a person is constantly bullied, abused or victimized as a child, he or she may grow up to be a bully themselves. Much of their outlook, values, personality and attitude will be shaped by these early childhood experiences or violence and abuse.

Many psychologists believe that a person is almost always drawn to things they inherently believe they lack to make up for it. For instance, people who are not sure of themselves or don't have a high self-confidence or self-esteem may constantly seek approval from others. They may look for approval and validation all the time.

Have you ever observed people who keenly attempt read their personality through zodiac signs or astrology? Isn't this a sign of possessing low self-awareness or understanding? People often gravitate towards things they believe they haven't got much of. For example, someone who hasn't been given sufficient attention by their parents during early childhood or teen years may grow up to be a person who thrives on drama and attention-seeking tactics. They may become more dramatic and showy.

There are plenty of clues everywhere. As a people analyzer, you just need to keep an eye out for these subtle clues.

Subconscious Mind and Human Behavior

Our mind is divided into three layers – the conscious mind, subconscious mind and unconscious mind. While the conscious mind or state of consciousness is awareness of thoughts, actions, learnings and experiences, the subconscious and unconscious mind are realms of the mind that hold things we may not be aware of.

Through the conscious mind, we have awareness of things we perceive and feel. We can process feelings, thoughts, concepts and ideas that are gathered from our immediate environment.

However, when it comes to the subconscious and unconscious mind, we have little or no awareness of the thoughts, ideas, concepts and information stored in it. Our conscious mind is only the tip of an iceberg. There are multiple hidden layers, which influence our personality and behavior that we are not aware of.

If you want to be a power-packed people analyzer, begin with yourself. Identify how much you know about yourself or how well you understand your own personality or behavior patterns. Attempt to understand what drives you into behaving in a specific manner. What are your underlying beliefs, fears, motivators, values and more?

Once you've uncovered your own personality and behavioral characteristics, attempt to understand close friends and family members. Lastly, move to strangers who you spot while waiting at a doctor's clinic or at the supermarket/airport or someone you've only just met at a party. Keep practicing to sharpen your people analyzing skills until you are able to read people quickly and effectively, like a pro!

Emotions and Human Behavior

Emotions are brief short conscious experiences that we experience as part of our mental activity. These feelings are not based in rational or logical thoughts. For example, even in the face of compelling proof that our friend is betraying us behind our back, we don't break ties with him or her and prefer to trust them.

As humans, we are prone to acting on impulses rather than logic, reasoning and evidence. People's behaviors are fundamentally shaped by emotions. Thus, understanding people's emotions gives us the power to comprehend and predict their actions, personality and behavioral patterns.

Chapter Two: Body Language and Voice Basics Revealed

Do you know that people communicate much more through what they leave unspoken than what they actually say? Body language accounts for around 55 percent of the entire message during the process of communication. In a study conducted by Dr. Albert Mehrabian, it was revealed that only 7 percent of our message is communicated through words, while 38 percent and 55 percent is conveyed through non-verbal elements such as vocal factors and body language, respectively.

Generally, what people say is well-thought and constructed within their conscious mind. This makes it easier to manipulate or fake words for creating a desired impression. Our body language, on the other hand, is guided by more involuntary movements of the subconscious mind. It is near impossible to fake subconsciously driven actions that we aren't even aware of. When you train yourself to look for non-verbal clues, you understand an individual's thoughts, feelings, actions and more at a deeper, subconscious level. Try controlling the thoughts held within your subconscious mind and you'll know what I am saying.

People are perpetually sending subconscious signals and clues while interacting with us, a majority of which we miss because we are conditioned to focus on their words. Since primitive times, human communicated through the power of gestures, symbols, expressions and more in the absence of a coherent language. You have the power to influence and persuade people through the use of body language on a deeply subconscious level since it's so instinctive and reflex driven.

Here are some of the most powerful body language decoding secrets that will help you unlock hidden clues held in the subconscious mind, and read people more effectively.

Establish a Behavior Baseline

Create a baseline for understanding a person's behavior if you want to read him or her more effectively. This is especially true when you are meeting people for the first time, and want to guard against forming inaccurate conclusions about people's behavior. Establishing a baseline guards you against misreading people by making sweeping judgments about their personality, feelings and behavior.

Establishing a baseline is nothing but determining the baseline personality of individual based on which you can read the person more effectively rather than making generic readings based on body language. For instance, if a person is more active, fast-thinking and impatient by nature, they will want to get a lot of things done quickly.

They may fidget with their hands or objects, tap their feet or appear restless. If you don't establish a baseline for their behavior, you may mistake their mental energy for nervousness or disinterest, since the clues are almost similar. You would mistakenly believe the person is anxious when he/she is hyperactive.

Observe and tune in to an individual completely to understand their baseline. This helps you examine both verbal and non-verbal clues in a context. How does a person generally react in the given situation? What is their fundamental personality? How do they communicate with other people? What type of words do they generally use? Are they essentially confident or unsure by nature?

When you know how they normally behave, you'll be able to catch a mismatch in their baseline and unusual behavior, which will make the reading even more effective.

Look For a Cluster of Clues

One of the biggest mistakes people make while analyzing others through non-verbal clues is looking for isolated or standalone clues instead of a bunch of clues. Your chances of reading a person accurately increases when you look at several clues that point to a single direction rather than making sweeping conclusions based on isolated clues. For instance, let us say you've read in a book about body language that people who resort to deception or aren't speaking the truth don't look a person directly in the eye.

However, it can also be a sign of being low on confidence or possessing low self-esteem. Similarly, a person may not be looking at your while speaking because he/she is directly facing discomfort causing sunlight. You ignore all other signs that point to the fact that the person is speaking the truth or is confident (a firm handshake, relaxed posture etc.) and only choose to look at the single clue that he/she isn't maintaining eye contact to inaccurately conclude that the person is lying. Look for at least 3-4 clues to arrive at a conclusion. Don't make sporadic conclusions about how a person is thinking or feeling based on single clues.

For all you know a person may be moving in another direction, not because they aren't interested in what you are speaking about or looking to escape, but because their seat is uncomfortable.

If you think the person is disinterested, look for other clues such as their expressions, gestures, eyes and more to make more accurate conclusions. Include a wider number of non verbal clues to make the analysis more accurate.

Look at the Context, Setting and Culture

Some body language clues are universal – think smile or eye contact. These signals more or less mean the same across cultures. However some non-verbal communication signals may have different connotations across diverse cultures.

For example, being gregarious and expressive is seen as common in Italian culture. People speak loudly, gesticulate with their hands in an animated manner, and are generally more expressive.

However, someone from England may decipher this behavior as massively exaggerated or a sign of nervousness. Enthusiasm, delight and excitement are expressed in a more subtle manner in

England. For the Italian, this retrained behavior may signify disinterest. While the thumbs-up is a gesture of good luck in the west, in certain Middle Eastern cultures it is viewed as rude. If you are doing business with people from across the world, understanding cultural differences before reading people is vital.

Similarly, consider a setting before making sweeping conclusions through non-verbal signs such as body language. For example, a person may display drastically different behavior when he's at work among co-workers, at the bar and during a job interview. The setting and atmosphere of a job interview may make an otherwise confident person nervous.

Head and Face

People are most likely experiencing a sense of discomfort when they raise or arch their eyebrows. The facial muscles also begin twitching when they are hiding something or lying. These are micro expressions that are hard to manipulate since they happen in split seconds and are subconscious involuntary actions.

Maintaining eye contact can be a sign of both honesty and intimidation/aggression. On the other hand, constantly shifting your gaze can be a non-verbal clue of deceit.

The adage that one's eyes are a window into their soul is true. People who don't look into your eyes while speaking may not be very trustworthy. Similarly, a shifting gaze can indicate nervousness.

The human eye movements are closely linked with brain regions that perform specific functions. Hence, when we think (depending on what or how we are thinking), our eyes move in a clear direction. For example, when a person is asked for details that he/she is retrieving from memory, their eyes will move in the upper left direction. Similarly, when someone is constructing information (or making up stories) instead of recalling it from memory, their eyes will shift to the upper right direction. The exact opposite is true for left-handed folks. When people try to recall information from memory, their eyes shift to the upper left, whereas when they try to create facts, the eyes move towards the upper left corner. A person who is making fictitious sounds or talking about a conversation that didn't happen, their eyes will move to the lateral left.

When there's an inner dilemma or conflict, a person's eyes will dart towards their left collarbone. This is an indication of an inner dialogue when a person is stuck between two choices. Increased eye movement from one side to another can signal deception. Again, look for a cluster of clues rather than simply analyzing people based on their eye movements.

Expanded pupils or increased blinking is a huge sign of attraction, desire and lust. A person may also display these clues when they are interested in what you are saying. If a person sizes you up by looking at you in an upward and downward direction, they are most likely considering your potential as a sexual mate or rival. Similarly, looking at a person from head to toe can also be a sign of intimidation or dominance.

When you are observing a person's face, learn to watch out for micro expressions that are a direct involuntary response based on feelings and thoughts. These reactions are so instinctive and happen in microseconds that they are impossible to fake. For example, when a person is lying, their mouth slants for a few microseconds and the eyes slightly roll.

How can you tell apart a genuine smile from a fake one? Pay close attention to the region around the person's eyes. If someone is genuinely happy, their smile invariably reaches their eye and causes the skin around the eyes to crinkle slightly. There are folds around the corner of the person's eyes if they are genuinely happy. Another clear sign of a genuine smile is a crow's feet formation just under the person's eyes. A smile is often used by people to hide their true feelings and emotions. It is near impossible to fake a smile (which is so involuntary and subconscious driven).

Even the direction of a person's chin can reveal a lot about their thoughts or personality. If their chin is jutting out, he/she may be a stubborn or obstinate about their stand.

Posture

When a person maintains an upright, well-aligned and relaxed posture, he/she is most likely in control of their thoughts and feelings and is confident/self-assured.

Their shoulders don't slouch awkwardly, and the overall posture doesn't sag. On the other hand, a sagging posture can be a sign of low self-esteem or confidence. It can also mean placing yourself below others or subconsciously begging for sympathy.

When a person occupies too much space physically by sitting with their legs apart or broadening their shoulders, they are establishing their dominance or power by occupying more physical space.

Limbs

Pay close attention to people's limb movements when you are reading them. When a person is bored, disinterested, nervous or frustrated, they will fidget with an object or their fingers. Crossing arms is a big signal of being, closed, suspicious, uninspired or in disagreement with what you are saying. The person isn't receptive to what you are speaking about.

If you want to get the person to listen to what you are saying, open them up subconsciously first by changing the topic of conversation. Once they are in a more receptive state of mind, resume the topic. When a person crosses their arms or legs, they are less likely to absorb or be persuaded by what you say.

A person's handshake can reveal a great deal about what they think about themselves or their equation with the other person. For instance, a weak handshake is a sign of nervousness, low self-esteem, lack of confidence, submissiveness and uncertainty. Similarly, a crushing handshake can be an indication of dominance or aggressiveness. A firm handshake implies self-confidence and a sense of self-assuredness.

Observe the direction in which a person's feet are pointed. If they are pointed in your direction, it means the person is interested in what you are saying. On the other hand, if they are pointed away from you, the person is looking for an escape route. Feet pointing in your direction or leaning slightly towards you are huge non-verbal signals of attraction.

Legendary Hollywood talent scouting agent once famously uttered, "I don't have a contract with my clients. Just a handshake is enough." You can indeed tell volumes about a person simply through their handshake.

Tone

The tone of a person's voice can communicate a lot about the way a person is feeling or thinking. Look for any inconsistency in a person's tone. Does the tone and pitch vary throughout the conversation? This can be a signal that the person is experiencing a surge of emotions. Listen to the volume of a person's voice. Something may not be quite right if they are speaking in a softer or louder than usual manner. Observe if the person is using filler words rather than concise phrases or sentences. It can be a sign of nervousness or they may be buying time to make up stories.

A person's tone can convey emotions they try to conceal or are unable to express. They may say something flattering to you but their tone may be slightly sarcastic or bitter, which can be a giveaway to what they are truly feeling. It can indicate a more passive aggressive personality. The meaning of exactly the same words can change drastically when delivered using a different tone, volume and inflection.

Let's say the person ends their sentence on a higher note. Doesn't it sound more like a question than a definitive statement? Similarly, if the person finishes their sentence on a flat note, he/she is making a confident or assured statement. The former can indicate doubt, uncertainty or suspicion, while the latter can be an indication of authority.

Proxemics

Proxemics refers to the physical space maintained during communication between people, which reveals volumes about how they relate to each other. Haven't you experienced a feeling of discomfort when someone tried to invade your personal space or come closer than you appreciate? This person is most likely seeking acceptance from you or trying to make their way into your inner social circle.

On the other hand, if a person comes closer than intended during negotiations, he/she may be trying to intimidate you or subconscious coax you into accepting their conditions. The ideal distance to test a person's comfort level is to stand at a minimum distance of four feet from them. If the person appears open, they are welcoming into their personal space. Similarly, if they are rigid, don't jump into their personal space immediately. They may not be ready to include you into their personal zone.

Mirroring

Mirroring a person's body language is a wonderful way to establish a rapport with a person on a subconscious level. Closely observe a person's body language while they are interacting with you. How is their posture? What are the words they typically use? If they are leaning against the bar or table, follow suit. Similarly, if they sip on their drink, mirror their action. If you spot them resting their elbow on a table, mirror their action.

Mirroring a person's action gives the other person an impression that you are one among them. It works on a primordial level to create sense of affiliation, likeliness and belongingness even before spoken language was invented. Adapt your actions, posture, gesture and movements with the other person to give a feeling of "being one among them." If the person is following your actions, they are seeking acceptance or validation from you.

Chapter Three: Reading People Through Personality Types

Personality analysis is a field that is constantly evolving and varied. There are varying schools of psychological thoughts and theories when it comes to studying an individual's personality. Some of the most popular personality analyzing schools include trait theory, social learning, biological/genetic personality influencer and more.

Personality refers to an individual's distinct characteristics connected to processing thoughts, feelings and emotions that eventually determine their behavior. It involves taking into consideration all the traits a person possess to understand them as an entity. Personality study also includes understanding the inherent differences existing between people where particular characteristics are concerned.

Here are some of the most common personality type classifications.

Type A, B, C and D

Type A personality people are at a bigger risk of contracting heart diseases since they are known to be more aggressive, competitive, ambitious, short-tempered, impatient, impulsive and hyper active. Type A personality theory was introduced in the 50's by Meyer Friedman and Ray Rosenman. These people are more stressed due to their constant need to accomplish a lot. They are always striving to be better than others, which invariably leads to greater anxiety and stress.

Type B people are more reflective, balanced, even-tempered, inventive and less competitive by personality. They experience less stress and anxiety, along with staying unaffected by competition or time constraints. A Type B personality person is moderately ambitious and lives more in the present. They have a steadier and more restrained disposition. Type B folks are social, modest, innovative, gentle mannered, relaxed and low on stress.

Later psychologists came up with other personality types, too, since they found the division into Type A and B more restrictive. They discovered that some people demonstrated a combination of both A and B Type traits. Thus, segregating people into only two distinct personality groups doesn't do justice to the classification. This lead to the creation of even more personality types!

Type C people have a more meticulous eye for detail. They are focused, curious and diplomatic. There tend to put other people's needs before theirs. They are seldom assertive, straightforward and opinionated. This leads to Type C folks developing pent up resentment, frustration, anxiety and depression. There is a propensity to take everything seriously, which makes them reliable and efficient workers.

This personality type also possess high analytic skills, logical thinking powers and intelligence. However, they need to develop the knack of learning to be less diplomatic and more assertive. Type C also needs to develop the ability to relax and let their hair down periodically.

Lastly, Type D personality people are known to hold a more pessimistic view of life. They are socially awkward and withdrawn, and do not enjoy being in the limelight. They are constantly worried about being rejected by people. Type D people are at a greater risk of suffering from mental illnesses such as depression owing to pessimism, pent up frustration and melancholy. Since the Type D personality doesn't share things easily with others, they suffer internally.

Psychoanalytic Theory

This theory is different from the regular personality classification theories in the sense that the analysis is based is not based on the responses of people about their personality, but a more in-depth study of people's personalities by glimpsing into their subconscious or unconscious mind. Since the analysis is based on a study on a person's subconscious mind, errors and instances of misleading the reader are eliminated.

In psychoanalysis, a person's words and actions are known to be disguised manifestations for their underlying subconscious emotions. The founding father of the psychoanalytic theory was Sigmund Freud, who was of the view that all human behavior is primarily driven by primitive instincts, passions, impulse and underlying emotions. He theorized that all human behavior is a direct consequence of the equation between our id, ego and superego.

Through the free association method that includes experiences, memories, dreams and more; Freud analyzed underlying emotions, thoughts and feelings that determine their attitude and behavior. Thus a majority of our behavior can be traced to our early childhood experiences that are still lingering in our subconscious mind, which we may or may not be aware of.

For example, if an individual demonstrates aggressive traits as an adult, it can be pinned down to the violence, harassment or bullying he/she experienced in their early childhood. Similarly, if a child comes from an environment where there were very high expectations from him/her and the parents were seldom happy with his/her accomplishments, he/she may constantly seek validation or acceptance from others. They may fear rejection.

Thus, a person's childhood experiences can help you determine their personality and read them even more effectively according to the psychoanalytic theory. The theory is still extensively used when it comes to helping people cope with depression, anger, stress, panic attacks, aggression, obsessive disorders and much more.

Carl Jung's Personality Classification Theory

Psychologist Carl Jung classified people on the basis on their sociability quotient into introverts and extroverts. Introverts are folks who are primarily inward driven, shy, withdrawn and reticent. They are more focused on their ideas and sensibilities than the external world around them. Introverts are known to be more logical, reflective and sensible by nature. They take time to crawl out of their box, and establish a rapport with others.

On the other hand, extroverts are outgoing, friendly, affable, social and gregarious people who live more in the present than worry about the future. They have a more positive and exuberant disposition, and are more than willing to accept challenges or changes.

After classifying people as introverts and extroverts, Jung received his share of brickbats from psychologists who believed that the classification was too restrictive to categorize every human being on the planet. Experts argued that a majority of people rarely demonstrated extreme introvert or extrovert tendencies. According to them only a majority of people possess extreme introvert or extrovert tendencies. Most people in fact possess a little bit of both, and their behavior differs according to the situation.

For instance, someone like me enjoys going out and spending time with people but I also value some time alone for reflection and contemplation every now and then. This neither makes me a hardcore extrovert or introvert but more of a combination of both – an ambivert.

Social Learning

This theory talks about how people pick up personality or behavioral traits from their immediate environment. It proposes that an individual's behavior is a result of their growing up conditions and environment. We pick up specific patterns and personality traits through our experiences. Social learning psychologists are of the view that all our behavior is learnt through our social experiences.

For example, if a person has been rewarded in a specific manner, he or she learns behavior through positive reinforcement and experiences. For example, someone throwing excessive tantrums may have learned through their experiences that drama gets them attention. Every time they want attention they know throwing tantrums will do the trick. At times, we don't have to experience something to learn behavior. Our mind is conditioned to use complex codes, information, actions, symbols and consequences. A majority of our observations and vicarious experiences drive our behavior, and help us imbibe specific personality traits.

Ernest Kretschmer's Classification

German psychologist Ernest Kretschmer's personality classification theory theorizes that a person's physical characteristics or personality traits determine the likelihood of a person suffering from mental ailments and their personality.

According to this personality classification, people are classified as Athletic, Pyknic, Dysplastic and Asthenic. Pyknic personality types are people who are round, stout and short. They demonstrate more extrovert traits such as gregariousness, friendliness and an outgoing disposition.

The Aesthetic personality types are people who have a slender and slim appearance. They have a fundamentally introvert personality. These are folks who have strong, athletic and robust bodies, and demonstrate more aggressive, enthusiastic and energetic characteristics.

Briggs Myers Personality Indicator

There are multiple personality tests that determine an individual's personality type based on a psychological analysis. One of the most widely used personality analysis tests is the Briggs Myers Personality Indicator. It is a comprehensive report that analyzes people's personalities based on how they perceive the world and make decisions.

The Briggs-Myers Personality Indictor was created by Isabel Briggs Myers and Katherine Briggs. It is based on Jung's theory but expounds on it through four primary psychological functions or processes such as sensation, thinking, feeling and intuition.

The MBTI emphasizes on one of the four primary functions dominating over other traits. The personality indicator operates on an assumption that everyone possesses a preference for the manner in which they experience the world around them. These inherent differences emphasize our values, motives, beliefs and interests, and thus determine an overall personality.

There are around 16 distinct personality types based on this psychological personality analysis theory. The Briggs-

Myers test comprises several questions, where test respondents reveal their personality through their answers. This test is also widely used in areas such as determining a person's chances of success in a particular role and compatibility in interpersonal relationships.

In Myers Briggs personality theory, a personality type is determined when there is a clear preference for one style over another. Different letters connected with individual preferences helps determine the person's Myers Briggs personality type. For instance, if a person reveals a clear tendency for I, S, T and J, they have the ISTJ personality type.

Extraversion and introversion – The first letter of the Briggs-Myers personality type is related to the direction of one's energy. If a person is externally focused or focused on the external world, they show a preference for extraversion. On the contrary, if the energy is inward directed, the person shows a clear inclination for introversion.

Sensing and Intuition – The second letter is concerned with processing information. If an individual prefers dealing with information, has clarity, can describe what they see etc. then they show a distinct preference for sensing. Intuition, on the other hand, is related to intangible ideas and concepts. Intuition is represented by the letter "N."

Thinking and Feeling – The third letter reflects an individual's decision making personality. People who show an inclination for analytic, logical and detached thinking reveal a tendency for thinking over feeling. Similarly, people who show a preference for feeling are more driven by their values or what they believe in.

Judgment and Perception – The last letter of the Briggs-Myer Type Indicator shows a person's way of viewing the world. If an individual reveals a preference for going with the tide and he/she is more flexible in their approach towards responding to things as they arise, they are perception driven. However, if their thoughts are more planned, rigid and clearly structured, they show an inclination for judging (judgment).

1. **INTJ – Introverted, Intuitive, Thinking and Judging**

    The INTJ personality type is primarily inventive, strategic, imaginative, resourceful and creative. They have a clear plan for everything. They are known to be original, analytical, independent thinking and resolute. They are good at planning, and executing plans into action. The INTJ personality type is perceptive when it comes to recognizing patterns and giving a clear logical reason for patterns.

They have a high sense of responsibility and commitment, and rarely quit something without completing it. They have high expectations not just from themselves but others too. The INTJ personality type makes for wonderful leaders, and also dedicated followers. These are generally the kind of people you want as original and independent thinking leaders.

2. ISTJ – Introverted, Sensing, Thinking, Judging

ISTJs are composed, quiet, reserved, serious and contemplative. They are primarily focused on living a secure, unruffled and peaceful life. These people are highly reliable, meticulous, disciplined, responsible and precision-oriented. They are logical, rational and practical. ISTJ folks possess a steady approach when it comes to fulfilling their objectives.

There is a deep respect for position, authority, establishment and a more conventional way of living. ISTJ people are concerned about maintaining order in their immediate physical space, work and life. If you are looking for administrators or managers for your business, these people may be a good fit.

3. ISFJ – Introverted, Sensing, Feeling, Judging

ISFJ people are quiet, kind, responsible conscientious. They are focused on fulfilling their responsibilities and obligations. There is a clear tendency for being practical, balanced and steady. They have an inherent need to place the feelings and needs of other people over theirs. ISFJ personality type people lean towards conventions and established norms. They don't believe in challenging customers, and are more concerned about leading a peaceful and secure life.

The ISFJ personality type is intuitively tuned in to the needs, emotions and feelings of other people. They have a deep service sense, and are suitable for vocations where they are needed to be of help to other people.

4. **ESTJ – Extroverted, Sensing, Thinking and Judging**

ESTJ people live in the moment, and have a high sense of appreciation for the present moment. They demonstrate a high sense of reverence for conventions, traditions and established customs, and they'll rarely go against it. ESTJ folks have a good idea about how things should be resolved speedily and effectively. This makes them a good fit for leadership positions. They are logical, rational, practical and innately realistic.

The ESTJ personality type excels at managing complex projects, and is focused on completing things with careful attention to details. They are reliable and dependable when it comes to accomplishing challenging tasks. The ESTJ personality type put in a lot into each task they undertake, which makes them efficient project managers or leaders. They place a lot of premium on law, justice, social order and security.

5. ISTP – Introverted, Sensing, Thinking and Perceiving

ISTP type people are inquisitive, curious and intelligent people who are always focused on knowing how everything works. They demonstrate a composed, peaceful and unruffled disposition. ISTP people also possess highly developed motor/mechanical skills and show an inclination for intense adventure. These people are more tolerant, flexible and adaptive by nature. They are excellent observers, people watchers and analyzers. ISTP folks are known to dive into the base of any situation before they come up with an actionable solution.

They will almost always emphasize on organizing facts, and establishing a precise cause and effect relationship. These are almost always the problem solvers, analyzers or solution providers that appear more logical and emotionally detached. Their solutions are more logically driven and less determined by emotions.

6. ISFP – Introverted, Sensing, Feeling, Perceiving

ISFP personality type people are shy, reflective, kind and sensitive. They avoid confrontation, arguments or heated conflict, and always focus on forming peaceful and harmonious relationships. ISFP people will avoid situations where there is scope for conflict. One distinct characteristic is the ISFP type's evolved sense of aesthetics. There is a higher tendency to be broadminded, adaptive and accommodating.

The ISFP folks aren't obstinate about their views, and posses a high sense of balance and appreciation for other people's views. They will agree to disagree with others in a graceful manner. ISFP type people are inventive, independent thinking and path-breaking original. They safeguard their space fiercely, and attempt to work within the given time frame with diligence. They live for the moment, and aren't too worked up about their future.

7. **ESTP – Extroverted, Sensing, Thinking, Perceiving**

ESTP personality type are outgoing folks who use a more rational, practical and logical approach while handling challenges. They focus on gaining fast results and solutions. ESTP people very efficient when it comes to analyzing people through multiple clues! They make for excellent psychologists, investigators and people analyzers. They are intuitive, and pick on both verbal and non-verbal clues effectively.

The ESTP personality type is action-oriented and practical, and prefers tangible actions over intangible ideas. They have a more problem solving, energetic, enthusiastic and proactive approach to life. They ESTP type people are more spontaneous, focused, random and attentive. Their ideal learning approach is hands on knowledge or learning by doing. They seek solutions by actively taking their problems head-on.

8. ESFP – Extroverted, Sensing, Feeling, Perceiving

ESTP type people are gregarious, flexible, amiable, loving and contemplative by nature. They seek new experiences, alternatives and possibilities. This personality type is also open for figuring out new ways to do things. They also like unique, unusual and off-beat stuff. These people are high on positivity and optimism.

They also make for exceptionally good team members, and love to combine their skills with other people to accomplish great results. These are folks who believe in living life queen or king size, while also developing solid relationships with others. The ESFP type is not very good when it comes to handling expectation, pressure and stress. They become pessimistic, negative and insecure.

9. ENTJ – Extroverted, Intuitive, Thinking and Judging

The ENTJ personality type is forthright, straightforward and outspoken, which makes them excellent leaders. According to them, the world is full of possibilities. Rather than perceiving problems as hurdles, they view them as challenges.

ENTJ personality type people are ambitious, practical, career-minded and solution oriented.

They will consider problems from several angles before coming up with practical, effective and workable solutions. The ENTJ personality type is in its element when it comes to goal setting and fulfilling these goals. The ENTJ personality type are outspoken, clear decision makers and effortless leaders. For these people, the world is full of possibilities.

They are well-read, knowledgeable, abreast with what is happening in the world and more aggressive when it comes to expressing their ideas. While they may not be too intuitively connected to other people's feelings, ENTJs can be surprisingly emotional.

10. INFP – Introverted, Intuitive, Feeling and Perceiving

The INFP personality type folks are balanced, composed, calm and contemplative. They are fiercely loyal and true to their value system. These people care deeply about others. They have a strong belief and value system, which guides them while making important decisions. The INFP people are loyal, adjusting, reliable, adaptable to change and relaxed. They easily empathize with other people, and reach to other people to make things easier for them.

11. INTP – Introvert, Intuitive, Thinking, Perceiving

INTP type people are independent thinking, creative, logical and analytic. They have a high sense of respect for knowledge and skills. By nature, they are reserved, reticent and withdrawn. They tend to exist in a world of their own and show little inclination for following others. The INTP personality type is fiercely independent and individualistic. They believe in creating their own route rather than following the one set by others.

12. ENFJ – Extroverted, Intuitive, Feeling and Judging

The ENFJ people have inherently well-developed people skills, and are known to be empathetic, kind, disciplined and affectionate. They are more externally focused and seldom enjoy being by themselves. The ENFJ people demonstrate an exceptional ability for spotting talent and skills in people. They also go out of the way to help people fulfill their real potential, thus making them wonderful leaders and managers.

One of the ENFJ personality type's best trait is their ability to accept praise and criticism with equal ease, while being faithful to people.

13. ESFJ – Extroverted, Sensing, Feeling and Judging

They ESFJ personality type are people who thrive when they are in the midst of other people. They are people persons, who enjoy interacting with other people, developing meaningful relationships with them, and getting to know them well. There is a huge need to be liked, admired and accepted by others. The ESFJ personality type desires that everything around them should be positive, balanced and harmonious for which they may go all out to support other people.

ESFJ people possess an inherent knack when it comes to making other people feel good about themselves. They will compliment and praise people lavishly in public, and ensure their strengths are highlighted. This personality type is popular because they have an inherent ability to make others feel special.

Their value or belief system is primarily guided by people around them, which makes them less rigid when it comes to their value system and beliefs. Also, they are more flexible when it comes to their different situations and persons. The ESFJ type enjoy being appreciated and are in their element when it comes to contributing to mankind's welfare. In any situation, they are concerned about the greater good.

14. ENTP – Extroverted, Intuitive, Thinking and Perceiving

The ENTP personality type is excited by ideas and concepts. They are able to analyze people and situations instinctively. They are fast decision makers and action takers. ENTP type people are also more alert, guarded, forthright and attentive. They are more fixated on possibilities or alternatives than plans.

They are excellent conversationalists who leave everyone bewitched with their words. ENTP don't like sticking to a routine, and are constantly seeking new experiences. They are experts at reading people, and have a deep sense of respect for learning. Again, they will consider multiple possibilities before zeroing down on a single solution.

15. ENFP – Extroverted, Intuitive, Feeling and Perceiving

The ENFP personality type people are fiercely independent, original and individualistic by nature. They believe in creating their own unique methods, habits, ideas, concepts and actions. This personality type doesn't fancy interacting with cookie clutter folks who follow the herd. They also despise being constrained in a box.

The ENFP personality type enjoys being around others and possess a strong sense of intuitive and sensitivity for others as well as themselves. They are more driven by emotions, and are known to be perceptive and contemplative. The ENFP personality type will think deeply about things from an emotional perspective before making a decision.

ENFP people are capable of accomplishing success in tasks that interest them. However, they also have a tendency to get easily bored doing things they aren't really good at. They don't fare too well when it comes to jobs that involve more meticulous, routine and detail-oriented tasks. They thrive in professions that allow them to express their creativity and come up with innovative ideas. Positions that are more confining and boxed will not appeal to them.

16. INFJ – Introverted, Intuitive, Feeling and Judging

The INFJ personality type are idealists, observers and visionaries who thrive on ideas and imagination. They have a unique and profound way of viewing the world. This personality type has the tendency to look at the world on a substantial and in-depth manner. They will seldom accept things as they are. While others view the INFJ personality as weird or eccentric, they stick to their unusual views about life.

The INFJ people are compassionate, caring, gentle and complex individuals who are more inclined towards creative, independent and artistic endeavors. They reside in a world that filled esoteric possibilities. While this personality type places a high premium of order and organization, they can also be surprisingly spontaneous and intuitive.

They will be able understand ideas intuitively without pinpointing the reason. This makes the INFJ people less organized and systematic than other judging personality types.

Chapter Four: Effectively Analyzing People Through Their Words

We don't use words mindlessly. There is a reason (often subconscious) behind our choice of words. The words we use are often guided by our subconscious feelings, emotions and thoughts. There is a clear underlying meaning behind phrases, words and other verbal expressions. Let us say for example, a person tells you that "Oh, so now you are dating another doctor." What does their choice of the word "another" indicate? It may imply that you just got out of a terrible relationship with a doctor, and fool hardily started dating another.

People use "yeah" and other similar terms when they want to communicate ambivalence. Similarly, they use "dude", "sis" or "bro" to express solidarity with people. It can be a sign of loyalty or friendship. There may also be a deep-seated need to be liked or accepted by the other person. People using these terms may seek to establish a sense of familiarity and belongingness with others. Begin by closely observing people's words and use it for peeking into the mind to unveil the thoughts and emotions behind their expressions.

Watch Out For Adjectives and Adverbs

The human brain is no short of a marvel. It is incredibly effective when it comes to thinking and vocalizing thoughts and/or ideas. When we think, our brains primarily use verbs and nouns. However, when we convert ideas or thoughts into language, we tend to elaborate on our thoughts by using adverbs and adjectives. These adverbs and adjectives that we use for describing basic nouns and verbs can reveal a lot about our inner feelings, thoughts and emotions.

They can also offer a glimpse into our predominant values, and other ideas.

For example, let us consider a sentence such as "I ate". It comprises a pronoun and action verb. The words or expressions used to modify these sentences can offer plenty of information about a person. These are modifying words that give clues into an individual's value system or behavioral patterns. Through verbal expressions or clues, you can make a fairly reliable guess about an individual's state of mind or character. If you add "fast" to the above sentence, it indicates urgency.

They may eat fast because they are late for a meeting or are conscious about being punctual. It can reveal a more commitment-driven, responsible, dedicated and disciplined approach. They have a deep sense of respect for social norms, and may be focused on other's expectations. They may be your ideal employees since they are fast, punctual and committed. Of course, there can be plenty of other reasons why a person eats fast. However, descriptive words can offer you a good indication about people's thoughts, behavior and overall values.

Read Between the Lines

Not everything people say reveals a lot about them. Often, what they leave unsaid also says a lot about them. Even when someone offers you a compliment such as "You are looking cool today", it may not go down well with you. To you it may imply that you are looking cool only today and not every day. We subconsciously tune in to what is left unsaid.

Let us take another example to understand the hidden meaning behind words or what people leave unsaid. You take your friends out a newly opened restaurant in your neighborhood. It's a much talked about place and you just can't wait to try the stuff there. As soon as you enter, the waiter/server greets you warmly and directs your group to the table.

What follows is an elaborate seven course meal. Before serving you each of the scrumptious courses, the waiter introduces each course and tells you interesting details about the preparations. You have a great time wining and dining with friends. Once you finish the entire seven course meal, you request the waiter to bring your check.

The waiter brings over your check and asks you for your feedback about the food. You sum it up in a single line by stating, "The soup was good." The waiter doesn't react too positively and looks a tad disappointed. You wonder why! According to you, you just paid him/her a compliment. However, the things you left unsaid revealed a lot about your opinion or thoughts regarding the food.

The other person subconsciously latched on to what you left unsaid. It revealed that apart from the soup, nothing else was worth mentioning or everything other than the soup was average. While people communicate plenty through what they say, they leave a lot of things unsaid.

I Test

This is yet another verbal determinant of an individual's personality. If a person uses the term "I" excessively, it indicates self-centeredness, selfishness or a large ego. However, the more "I" a person uses, the less powerful he/she feels. People who aren't sure about their power feel the desire to establish false sense of power through excessive usage of "I." Do a tiny exercise right now. Browse through the mails that are sent by people in a position of high authority. Now compare these mails will people who aren't in very authoritative positions, you'll clearly notice more usage of "I" in the latter.

For example, "Dear Jones, I was a student of your biology class last year. I have always enjoyed being a part of your classes. I've learned a lot through them. I received an email from you related to research collaboration. I would really appreciate working with you." Mr. Jones may reply with "That's amazing news. This week may be slightly busy for me owing to prior commitments. How about a meeting next Tuesday from 5 to 7? It will be wonderful to catch up."

Other than an indication of less power and higher self consciousness, it is also a clue of depression. A research published in Scientific Study of Literature revealed that illustrious poets who committed suicide frequently resorted to the usage of first-person pronouns while writing poetry.

Talking About Others

What people say about other people is often a reflection of their own personality. In a research conducted by Siminie Vazire and Peter Harms, it has been discovered that asking people to rate others on three negative and three positive aspects gave plenty of insights about their social personality, overall being, mental health and their view about others. It was found that a person's tendency to see others in a more positive light indicates their own positivity.

There is a powerful link between having an opinion about other people and possessing an energetic, courteous, optimistic, emotionally balanced and kind personality. Talking positively about other people demonstrates how positively they view their own lives. On the other hand, people who use unflattering and negative words and phrases view themselves in an inferior light.

There is a greater correlation between using unflattering words used for describing other people and narcissism, low self-confidence, anti-social tendencies, frustration, overall dissatisfaction and more. People with a primarily negative personality type tend to view others in a more unflattering light. This can be a strong indication of mental issues, personality disorder or an unstable mind.

The Object Description Analysis

The manner in which a person describes an object is also enough to give you a fair idea about how the individual views the world, along with how he/she thinks and feels. The most commonly used cluster words will offer a clear basis for their behavior and personality. This linguistic personality determination technique is called meaning extraction.

Additional Words

The extra or additional words a person uses while conversing with you can reveal a lot about their thoughts, behavior and personality. For example, if someone says, "I won yet another award" in place of "I won an award", it reveals a need to tell people that they've won plenty of awards earlier. The individual may be struck with a terrible complex that makes them scream about their objection from rooftops.

Pick up this clue and learn that one of the best ways to develop a rapport with this person is to hail them for their accomplishments. Their words present an area of weakness that you can quickly cash on. Watch out for an incompatibility between the person's verbal and non-verbal clues. For example, an individual may state that they are delighted to meet you. However, if their body language is rigid, inflexible and uncomfortable, something may be wrong. A trained eye can easily figure out inconsistencies between a person's verbal and non-verbal signals.

You can fall back on their words and body language collectively to understand what the person is thinking or feeling.

"I Made Up My Mind" – Introverts and Extroverts

If an individual says he/she has made up their mind, they have most likely considered several options before making a clear decision. It implies that a person is prone to contemplating and reflecting upon their decision rather than making spur of the moment decisions. They have deliberated on their decision, and may be analytic or logical by nature.

There are lesser chances of them being rash, spontaneous and impulsive decision makers. The words are an indication of a person's introvertedness and extrovertedness. Taking decisions after giving it a thought is a sign of introvertedness.

However, guard against making instant, sporadic decisions about people based on the words they use. Simply using "decided" or "I made up my mind" isn't enough to make conclusions about an individual's personality. Identify a clear pattern and several verbal/non-verbal clues to read people more effectively. Watch out for clues that support your initial reading or point to contrary evidence.

Extroverts collect their energies from other people and their environment. They stimulation and decision making comes from using the trial and error technique over reflectively contemplating on their decision. Extroverts may speak more spontaneously without thinking, while introverts will carefully weight their words and its implications.

You can tailor your own communication pattern to suit the other person's once you get to know if they are an introvert or extrovert. Identifying whether a person is an introvert or extrovert helps you understand how someone makes decisions. For example, let us say you are selling insurance. You may have to determine what drives both the introvert and extrovert personality types to make a decision about buying insurance.

Introverts may be more reflective and mull over the options before making a decision, while extroverts are more prone to making quick decisions. If you notice a primarily introverted mindset, give people more time to think before making a decision. Pushing these folks to make a quick decision may backfire. They may get uncomfortable with the idea of being pushed into a decision.

If you are negotiating important businesses deals, you don't give introverts enough time to mull over the conditions, they may come up with a negative response. On the contrary, people who make fast decisions show sign of being extroverts. They can be pushed into making fast decisions. However, one of the most vital things to keep in mind is that people rarely demonstrate absolute introvert or extrovert tendencies. A majority of people are a combination of introvertedness and extrovertedness.

Chapter Five: Personality and Birth Order

An individual's birth order can also reveal a lot of his or her personality. This isn't just restricted to pop psychology talk or mindless party chatter but based on a psychological analysis of how the person relates to their family members and how they are treated within the family based on their position or birth order. A person's family dynamics plays a considerable role in shaping their personality. The role they fulfilled as children or during their adolescent years influences their behavior as adults. Our status quo as children establishes the foundation for our actions as adults. Notice how several times children born in the same family or raised in the same environment have dramatically diverse personalities.

Of course, there are other factors that in combination with a person's birth order can determine their personality type. These factors such as the family's overall socio-economic status, education, number of children in the family, parent's professional achievements and more also impacts an individual's personality.

It was Alfred Adler who first came up with the theory of studying an individual's personality through their birth rank. He used it a method for reading the behavior, personality and actions of his clients. However, it was Frank Sulloway who elaborated on the theory in his publication *Born to Rebel.* Sulloway's book identified five primary traits like extraversion, agreeableness, neuroticism, consciousness and openness.

The psychologist mentioned that an individual's birth order impacts their personality even more than their environment. This means that the chances of two first-borns having the same personality type is higher than two children belonging to one family.

Here are some ways to read a person through their birth order.

First-borns

First born children are known to be responsible and ambitious leaders, who pave the way for others. They are original, creative and independent thinking by nature. Since they get more undivided attention and time with their parents, they have a clear edge over their siblings. Again, they are more proactive and take the lead when it comes to caring for the siblings, which makes them more disciplined, inspiring, responsible and accountable as adults. They are protective towards those weaker than them, and often lead others.

If parents place a lot of expectations on the first in a household, the person may grow up feeling inadequate. This may not just lead to low self esteem but also a weak personality that is marked by a constant need for validation, acceptance and approval. The person may end up feeling that they can never be good enough for anything.

First born individuals are more goal-oriented and ambitious. They give plenty of importance to accomplishments and success. They thrive in or perform well in positions of authority, responsibility and maintaining discipline. There is an inherent tendency to be a control freak, while also being autocratic, dictatorial and bossy.

Owing to the fact that come first in the sibling hierarchy, these people are physically stronger than other children in the household, which gives them a marked dominant personality. They may have a high sense of entitlement.

First-borns are often high on determination, rule enforcement and attention to details.

Middle-borns

Since they are caught between two siblings, middle-borns develop a more complicated personality. They are neither given the rights and responsibilities of the older sibling nor the special privileges of the youngest sibling. This makes them look outside the home for friendships and connections.

Middle-borns often have very big social circles and are known to be excellent diplomats and negotiators. They are social creatures who function with a profound sense of peace and fairness. Middle-borns are fiercely loyal to their loves ones and seldom betray people's trust. Typical personality traits of middle born children are flexibility, generosity and adaptability. They are known for their diplomatic nature, and can play peacemakers in any situation.

Middle born children are primarily understanding, co-operative and adjusting. They also turn out to be competitive adults. Middle-borns have a close-knit social circle who award them the affection they haven't received within their family. Middle-borns are late raisers, and discover their calling after plenty of experimentation, contemplation and deliberation. They are at the center of authoritative careers that allow them to utilize their power-packed negotiation skills.

Middle-borns are generally social and operate with a deep sense of justice and fairness. Their typical personality characteristics include generosity, diplomacy, flexibility and adaptability.

They are good at teamwork, and relate well with people belonging to multiple personality types since they have learnt to deal with older and younger siblings. Middle-borns display a more affable nature, and they know how to wriggle themselves out of confrontations and conflicts. They are known to be resourceful and quickly master multiple skills.

Last Born

By the time the youngest child of the family is born, parents are well-versed in their parenting skills and more economically settled. This makes them less paranoid and more secure. They aren't excessively monitored, which makes them more independent and freedom. Last born are excellent decision makers, and operate with a high sense of entitlement.

The last born is known to be charming and risk taking. They are independent thinking, original and adventurous. There is a greater tendency to rewrite the rules rather than following set norms.

Parents are less careful when it comes to their last born because they've already experienced being a parent, which helps them give more leeway and flexibility to the youngest child. Also, there are higher chances of pampering and indulging the child owing to a better financial status. Since parents are more relaxed and lenient with last-borns, they don't turn out to be conformists. They are used to plenty of attention, and they don't worship authority.

Rather than walking on set paths, they will create their own path. Since they've learnt to compete with their siblings for their parent's time and attention, they are good are handling competition and aren't easily bothered by feelings of envy and insecurity.

Since they are more creative and independent thinking, they thrive in careers such as stand up comedians, painters, dancers and authors. Typical personality characteristics include empathy, obstinacy, extroversion, manipulativeness, penchant for drama and more. These are your salespeople, since they are glib and can talk themselves of almost any situation.

Sole Child

The only child doesn't have to complete with anyone for their parents' time and attention, which makes them self-centered. There is a tendency to think that everything revolves around them. They tend to spend a lot of time alone, which turns them into more original, resourceful, inventive and creative people. Sole or only children find new and innovative ways to keep themselves busy. By nature, they are more confident, self-assured, meticulous, expressive and firm. They express their opinions more assertively and confidently.

Since they do not have to deal with sibling rivalry of any kind, they are always used to having things their way. They become edgy and unsettled when they have to complete with others or things don't go their way. Sole-borns find it tough to share the limelight with others. They almost always want to be the center of attention since they've never had to complete with any for attention at home through their childhood and adolescent years. Only-borns are constantly seeking attention, respect and attention. In the absence of siblings as role models, their only role models are elders of the house. Since grown-ups become their role models, they grow up to be perfectionists.

There are multiple factors that impact a person's behavioral characteristics and personality. To make a more accurate reading an individual's personality through birth order, there are some effective tips offers by psychologists. They recommend analyzing a person's siblings while reading their personality since no two children in the same household ever share the same role. If one assumes the role of a caretaker, the other will invariably be the care recipient.

Other factor that are taken into consideration while analyzing an individual's personality through birth order is genetics, gender, social status and other factors (apart from their birth order). These factors together will help you make more accurate readings about an individual's personality than simply relying on birth order.

Conclusion

I genuinely hope this book has offered you multiple invaluable insights about reading people's personality through well-researched strategies, tried and tested techniques and a bunch of practical tips. These tips can be applied in just about any situation from professional to interpersonal relationships to your social life.

Whether you want to figure out the personality of a prospective buyer during a negotiation or the personality traits of the new date you have your eyes on, this book is a valuable resource for helping you read others effectively. If there's a single largest skill that translates into success in modern times, it is the knack of reading people.

When you know how a person thinks or feels, you can mould your message according to his or her personality for accomplishing an optimally beneficial outcome.

The next step is to use this book and apply it in your everyday life in tiny, gradual ways to start with. Begin by observing people at the airport, supermarket or doctor's clinic when you have free time. You'll become more interested in the art of analyzing people, and find yourself doing it at every given opportunity.

Finally, if you enjoyed reading the book, please take the time to share your views by posting a review of Amazon. It'd be highly appreciated!

47293326R00059

Made in the USA
Columbia, SC
30 December 2018